The Entrepreneurial Mindset

Building Mental Strength for Success

Table of Contents

Chapter 1. Introduction

Embark on an exciting journey of self-discovery and empowerment with our Special Report, "The Entrepreneurial Mindset: Building Mental Strength for Success". This enlightening piece will not only give you a comprehensive insight into the powerful entrepreneurial mindset but will also steer you towards developing the mental fortitude key in steering your dream venture towards greater success. Filled with inspiring stories, practical tips, and actionable strategies, this Special Report is your springboard to exploring untapped potentials and reaching the zenith of entrepreneurial success. Intrigued? Supercharge your entrepreneurial journey by investing in this treasure trove of wisdom and watch as your business aspirations come alive like never before.

Chapter 2. Understanding the Entrepreneurial Mindset

The entrepreneurial mindset doesn't just spring into existence suddenly, but rather is molded and honed over time by various experiences, significant learnings, unrelenting perseverance, and thorough introspection. It functions similar to a lens, providing a unique perspective that aids in identifying opportunities, innovatively solving problems, and directing consistent efforts towards maintaining a solution-oriented approach and creating value.

2.1. The Anatomy of an Entrepreneurial Mindset

The entrepreneurial mindset can be elucidated by delving into several innate characteristics that fuel the entrepreneurial drive in individuals.

Indispensable Optimism: Undeterred by adverse circumstances, an entrepreneur often exudes a positive outlook, enthusiastically working towards their goals. After all, optimism is not a mere passive expectation of good things, but a radiant, motivating force that compels action.

Persistence: It can often make the difference between defeat and victory. Even when faced with setbacks, an entrepreneur's persistent belief in their idea and themselves keeps them on the trail to success.

Passion: A deeply ingrained love for one's work or product is a profound catalyst that can drive a venture forward, even amid challenges.

Risk Tolerance: Entrepreneurs maintain the ability to proceed despite the likelihood of failure, showing courage to endure the unknown while continuously striving for success.

2.2. Willingness to Learn

Beyond the above traits, successful entrepreneurs are lifelong learners. They recognize that maintaining a successful business isn't a one-and-done achievement, but rather an ongoing evolution that requires the constant acquisition of knowledge. They avidly read, relentlessly network, seek mentoring opportunities, and engage in various learning platforms to stay updated in their fields.

2.3. Intrinsic and Extrinsic Motivation

Entrepreneurs are often fueled by both intrinsic motivation, such as creative fulfillment or a strong desire to facilitate a positive social impact, and extrinsic motivation like fiscal rewards and public recognition. This blend of motivations can empower them to spearhead their businesses through obstacles and to greater heights.

2.4. The Entrepreneur's Perspective on Failure

Instead of viewing failure as a final endpoint, successful entrepreneurs interpret it as an integral part of their entrepreneurial journey. They value each setback as an opportunity to enhance their business strategy, develop resilience, and refine their maneuvers for subsequent ventures.

2.5. Perseverance Is Key

An entrepreneurial journey is often strewn with challenges. So, it's essential to not just possess a strong willpower but also judge when to pivot or tweak a faulty approach. Perseverance and adaptability can often coexist, propelling the venture towards its envisioned success.

2.6. Cultivating Your Entrepreneurial Mindset

The good news is that an entrepreneurial mindset doesn't come with one's DNA; it can be cultivated.

Visualize Success: Visualizing enables you to keep your efforts aligned with your goal, fostering tenacity amidst setbacks.

Continuous Learning: Dedicate time every day for learning, be it from books, networking events, mentors, or online courses. Upgrade yourself with the latest industry trends and insights.

Embrace Failure: Treat failure as a critical learning tool. Remember, every unsuccessful attempt is just one step closer to success.

Seek Mentors: Find someone who inspires you and can provide valuable industry insights, guidance, and support. This can significantly alleviate the journey's hardships.

Practice Optimism: Ensure that you focus more on constructive thoughts rather than on demotivating ones. It can help foster a positive work environment and enable steadier progress.

Hone Resilience: Develop strategies that help you bounce back from setbacks. Remember, resilience is the wind beneath the wings of an entrepreneurial endeavor.

The entrepreneurial mindset is a formidable tool that can be invaluable in garnering success in your entrepreneurship journey. At its core, this mindset is about courage, risk-taking, perseverance, lifelong learning, and a relentless pursuit of opportunities. While such qualities may seem daunting to develop, remember that every journey begins with a single step. So, take that first step today, cultivate your entrepreneurial mindset, and steer your venture towards the limitless heights of success. Remember, the sky is not the limit but only the beginning!

Chapter 3. The Role of Persistence in Achieving Success

In the world of entrepreneurship, adaptability, innovation, and vision are widely-known prerequisites for success. However, there exists an underrated, yet intrinsic trait within successful entrepreneurs, one that separates the dreams from reality — Persistence. Delving deep into the vital role of persistence can begin to unveil its impact on entrepreneurial success.

3.1. Persistence - The Key to Overcoming Entrepreneurial Roadblocks

The journey of entrepreneurship is scattered with roadblocks, often unexpected, that threaten to stall progress and douse the flames of motivation. When faced with such roadblocks, it is persistence that gears the entrepreneur to face the challenges head-on, steadfast in their determination to overcome them. Each roadblock conquered paves the way for learning and growth, thus fortifying the venture and leading it towards the path of success.

3.2. Learning from Persistent Notables

Many renowned entrepreneurial figures exemplify the virtue of persistence. Walt Disney, the creative genius behind The Walt Disney Company, had been fired by a newspaper editor for lacking imagination and had numerous business ventures fail before he finally hit big with Mickey Mouse. Thomas Edison, the brilliant inventor of the electric light bulb, had endured a staggering 10,000 failures before he finally succeeded. These instances are a testament to how persistence can turn repeated failures into monumental success.

3.3. The Psychology Behind Persistence

From a psychological perspective, persistence arises from the concept of self-efficacy — the belief in one's capabilities to orchestrate and execute courses of action required to manage prospective situations. Self-efficacious entrepreneurs have conviction in their abilities and are willing to persist longer, contributing significantly to their success.

3.4. The Art of Fostering Persistence

Fostering persistence may seem daunting, but it essentially involves cultivating the right mindset. Instilling the belief that failures are stepping stones to success, being visionary in setting long-term goals, and nurturing resilience and tenacity can help fuel persistence.

Finding a mentor who can guide, give unbiased feedback, and provide encouragement during challenging times can also significantly foster persistence. Surrounding oneself with the right mindsets, such as network of persistent and successful entrepreneurs, can further foster an environment of persistence.

3.5. Role of Persistence in Decision Making

Persistence plays a crucial role in decision-making, particularly in scenarios where making or breaking is contingent on timing. Persistent entrepreneurs are not daunted by short-term failures or setbacks; rather, they view them as learning opportunities, making them better equipped to make proactive and wise business decisions in the future.

3.6. Persistence and Adaptability

While persistence is critical, it should not equate to stubbornness. An entrepreneur should be willing to adapt as per the demands of the evolving market landscape. Hence, a balance of persistence to stay the course, complemented with adaptability to adjust the sails as per the shifting winds of the market, is vital for entrepreneurial success.

3.7. The Harmony of Persistence and Passion

The synergy of passion and persistence holds immense power. Passion fuels the drive to create, innovate, and lead, while persistence ensures that the entrepreneur remains undeterred by impediments. The combination of both forms an unstoppable force that can propel an entrepreneurial venture to new heights.

3.8. Closing Thoughts

Success in entrepreneurship is a marathon, not a sprint. Persistent entrepreneurs persevere despite countless setbacks, leveraging their failures into learning experiences. It is the relentless pursuit of their vision coupled with adaptability and a passionate drive that ultimately enables them to achieve their entrepreneurial goal.

In sum, persistence is more than just a mere quality; it is a mindset that needs to be nurtured, a weapon to be wielded, and a beacon that illuminates the path to entrepreneurial success. The role of persistence in achieving success, as such, cannot be overstated. Therefore, always be persistent, for persistence is the lifeblood of entrepreneurship.

Chapter 4. Cultivating Fearlessness in Business

The pathway to entrepreneurial success is often fraught with uncertainties and challenges that demand a unique blend of courage and vulnerability. Cultivating fearlessness in business is, therefore, integral to nurturing the entrepreneurial mindset.

4.1. Understanding Fear and Its Impact on Business

Fear, in the context of entrepreneurship, is often marked by a dread or avoidance of potential adverse circumstances that could arise within the business realm. At its root, entrepreneurial fear often stems from a concern of failure, financial loss, or the idea of one's business venture not meeting success. This worry often manifests as hesitation in decision-making, avoidance of risks, or, in some instances, complete stagnation in business growth.

Understanding the impact fear can have on your business ventures is crucial to developing fearlessness. A business journey shrouded in fear and apprehension can lead to missed opportunities, lack of innovation, and the potential downfall of an otherwise promising venture. Addressing these fears is the first step towards cultivating fearlessness.

4.2. Developing an Attitude of Fearlessness

Fostering an attitude of fearlessness fundamentally marks a shift from a reactionary mindset to a proactive one. Fear often prompts individuals to react defensively to adversities, while fearlessness encourages a proactive approach, focusing on generating solutions rather than dwelling on problems.

1. Start with Self-Awareness: Evaluate your current mindset and acknowledge your fears. This self-awareness allows you to recognize the areas that demand courage and assertiveness.

2. Embrace Positivity: Develop a positive mindset that can help reshape your perception of fear and risk. Positive affirmations, regular reflection and meditation can aid in fostering optimism.

3. Adopt Resilience: Make resilience a practice. The journey may be rough, but with a resilient mindset, you can quickly bounce back from any setback.

4.3. Embracing Risk and Uncertainty

Risk and uncertainty are inherent parts of the business world. As such, they are often seen as sources of fear among entrepreneurs. However, with the proper mindset, you can transform these aspects into opportunities for growth and innovation.

Inclining towards calculated risks and embracing uncertainty can help expand your business and lead to breakthroughs that might not have been possible within a rigid, fear-based framework. It's not about being reckless; it's about making informed decisions and taking measured actions, even when the outcome is uncertain. This opens a world of possibilities and takes you closer to your entrepreneurial vision.

4.4. Channeling Fear into Motivation

While the ultimate goal is to cultivate fearlessness, the presence of fear isn't entirely detrimental. When channeled correctly, fear can serve as a potent motivator that fuels your drive to succeed.

It's about recognizing the difference between debilitating fear and healthy fear. The former paralyzes you, preventing progress. The latter, however, can motivate you to take action and avoid potential failure. Identifying the underlying fears and leveraging them as springboards for success is a key aspect of cultivating fearlessness in business.

4.5. Conclusion: Reinforcing Fearlessness in Business Practices

Cultivating fearlessness isn't an overnight process; it's a gradual journey that requires time, patience, and consistent efforts. It's about fostering a mindset that ushers in it an unwavering vision for success, undeterred by the mere prospect of failure or adversity.

Incorporating practices like cognitive behavioral therapy, meditation, and mentorships can help reinforce an attitude of fearlessness. Building a supportive network of mentors, colleagues and like-minded individuals who have faced similar fears can be immensely reassuring.

Remember, fearlessness is not the absence of fear. It is the audacity to proceed with courage, determination, and a belief in your abilities, even when the path ahead is uncertain. Armed with a fearless attitude, no challenge is too large, no dream too ambitious, and no goal unattainable.

Chapter 5. Risk-Taking: A Fundamental of Entrepreneurship

Risk-taking acts as the lifeblood of entrepreneurship. Entrepreneurs often find themselves standing at the precipice of uncertainty and potential failure. Yet, it is this very ability to take calculated risks that aids them in leapfrogging their competition and carving out successful business ventures.

5.1. The Essence of Risk in Entrepreneurship

Risk is not just inherent to the entrepreneurial process; it epitomizes its very essence. In its simplest form, risk represents the potential for loss. However, for the entrepreneur, risk also holds the thrilling promise of unprecedented reward. Every decision taken, from pivoting a business strategy to launching an innovative product, courting a new market or even quitting a stable day job to dive headfirst into the start-up waters, carries a potential for gain, as well as the perilous possibility of loss. This delicate balance between risk and reward underpins the dynamic world of entrepreneurship, driving innovative solutions and disruptive breakthroughs.

When entrepreneurs shoulder risk, they subject their time, capital, and social equity to possible detriment. However, these risks also act as catalysts for innovation, urging entrepreneurs to venture beyond familiar confines, explore unfamiliar territories and find novel ways to solve problems. The ethos of entrepreneurship thrives amid the ebb and flow of uncertainty.

5.2. Understanding the Types of Risks

For better decision-making and preparing effective risk management strategies, entrepreneurs need to cognize the different types of risks in entrepreneurship.

1. **Financial Risk:** This is the most common risk associated with entrepreneurship. It is the possibility of monetary loss, often stemming from a failing business, inadequate cash flow, or financial challenges, such as market fluctuations or loan repayments.

2. **Product Risk:** This risk arises when there's a lack of demand for the product or service offered. Constant market research, customer insights, and product analysis can help mitigate this risk.

3. **Team Risk:** Building a cohesive team that effectively works towards a common goal is essential. However, internal conflicts, lack of commitment, or inadequate skills can disrupt this harmony, leading to team risks.

4. **Market Risk:** Unexpected industry trends, changing customer preferences, or sector volatility can prove to be significant market risks. Market research, analysis, and regular updates can help entrepreneurs navigate market risks.

Entrepreneurs' understanding of these risks can help them devise robust strategies and mechanisms to weather unforeseen circumstances and to keep moving forward, even when faced with adversity.

5.3. Embracing Ambiguity: An Entrepreneurial Imperative

A prerequisite for risk-taking in entrepreneurship is cultivating comfort with ambiguity. After all, entrepreneurship often represents sailing unchartered waters where market reactions, customer behavior, and industry trends can be unpredictable. The ability to make decisions despite ambiguities and limited information is what sets entrepreneurs apart.

The entrepreneurial journey is fraught with inherent uncertainties - the success of new products, the entry of competitors, shifts in the industry, changes in governmental regulation, or fluctuations in the economy. However, entrepreneurs who are comfortable with ambiguity can maintain a clear-headed focus amidst these uncertainties, allowing them to capitalize on opportunities while their competition hesitates.

5.4. Calculated Risk-Taking: The Entrepreneurial Approach

Unlike the often-misunderstood concept of entrepreneurs being reckless risk-takers, seasoned entrepreneurs understand the importance of calculated risks. They view risks from a balanced perspective — they are neither overly cautious that they miss opportunities, nor highly impulsive that they plunge into unwise ventures.

Calculated risks involve a thorough understanding of the problem, meticulous analysis, weighing of possible outcomes, risk mitigation strategies, and above all, the readiness to counteract and adapt if things don't align as per plans. The difference between successful entrepreneurs and others often lies in their ability to think through these parameters while making decisions.

5.5. Risk Mitigation Strategies

Entrepreneurship doesn't mean the blind acceptance of risks. Instead, it pertains to the identification, evaluation, and mitigation of risks. Below are some strategies that can help entrepreneurs manage risks:

Understand the Market: Comprehensive market research provides invaluable insights into the industry trends, customer preferences, competitor strategies, and potential opportunities or threats. These insights form the basis of strategic decision-making and can greatly reduce market and product risks.

Diversify: Don't put all your eggs in one basket. By having diverse product lines, servicing multiple market segments, or investing in different businesses, entrepreneurs can spread their risk and safeguard against unexpected downturns.

Build a Strong Team: A competent and committed team acts as an entrepreneur's defense line against risks. By investing in the right human capital, fostering a culture of learning and adaptation, and maintaining a high level of team morale, entrepreneurs can navigate through various hurdles.

Risk Transfer: Insurance is a vital tool for transferring risk. Whether it's property insurance, liability insurance, or insurance of key individuals, it helps cover losses if a risk eventuates.

5.6. Nurturing Mental Strength for Risk-Taking

Risk-taking can put significant pressure on entrepreneurs. Hence, mental fortitude is a crucial attribute when navigating this stress-inducing journey. Elements of mental strength in entrepreneurship involve cultivating resilience, maintaining a positive attitude even in difficult times, staying persistent despite setbacks, and being flexible to adapt to changing scenarios. It's a mix of emotional intelligence, mental resilience, adaptive thinking, and an undying spirit of exploration.

To sum up, risk-taking isn't about plunging headlong into every opportunity. Effective risk-taking in entrepreneurship is about understanding the balance between risk and reward, making informed decisions, implementing robust risk mitigation strategies, and maintaining resiliency and adaptability in the face of adversity.

Chapter 6. Developing Emotional Intelligence for Business Improvement

Emotional intelligence, often referred to as EQ (Emotional Quotient), is the ability to understand, use and manage our own emotions in positive ways to relieve stress, communicate effectively, empathize with others, overcome challenges and defuse conflict. Emotional intelligence impacts many different aspects of your daily life, such as the way you behave and interact with others. If you have high emotional intelligence, you are able to recognize your own emotional state and the emotional states of others, and engage with people in a way that draws them to you.

6.1. Understanding Emotional Intelligence

The concept of emotional intelligence was first popularized by psychologists John D. Mayer and Peter Salovey in the early 1990s. They defined it as the ability to perceive and express emotion, absorb emotion in thought, understand and reason with emotion, and regulate emotion in oneself and others.

In the context of entrepreneurship, understanding your emotions, as well as those of your employees, clients, and competitors, can create a substantial competitive edge. This can lead to stronger relationships, better decision making, and increased resilience. Developing your emotional intelligence can take time, but starting with simple steps might help you build an emotionally intelligent business.

6.2. Role of EQ in Business

High emotional intelligence helps you understand and manage your emotions, which can lead to better decision making and problem-solving. It can also help you navigate social complexities of the workplace, lead and motivate others, and excel in your job performance.

When you have the ability to manage your emotions and understand those of others, you become a person people want to follow. This is critical for entrepreneurs who are continually looking for ways to motivate their team and foster a workplace culture that supports high performance and engagement.

6.3. Building Emotional Intelligence

Building emotional intelligence doesn't happen overnight. It requires time, patience, and consistent effort. Here are some ways to develop your own emotional intelligence:

1. Self-awareness: The first step to developing emotional intelligence is self-awareness. This involves being aware of your own emotional state, and recognizing your triggers and responses. By understanding what causes you to feel certain emotions, you can better manage those emotions and avoid reactive behavior.

2. Self-regulation: This involves managing your actions in response to your emotions. It means understanding that you have a choice in how you react to situations.

3. Motivation: Motivated people are more likely to have high emotional intelligence because they have a strong drive to achieve, are optimistic even during setbacks, and are committed to their work.

4. Empathy: Understanding what others are feeling is a key aspect

of emotional intelligence. Empathy not only helps you understand people better, but it also helps you build stronger relationships.

5. Social skills: This includes skills like communication, managing relationships, leadership, and influence. People with strong social skills are skilled at managing relationships to move people in a desired direction.

6.4. Encouraging Emotional Intelligence in the Workplace

As a business leader, you have the unique opportunity to foster an emotionally intelligent culture within your organization. You can do this through various strategies:

1. Lead by example: One of the most effective ways to foster emotional intelligence within your team is to model it yourself.

2. Provide training and development: Consider implementing training programs or workshops focused on enhancing emotional intelligence. These programs can provide practical techniques for improving empathy, self-awareness, and emotional regulation.

3. Encourage open communication: Promoting a culture where employees feel comfortable expressing their feelings can help foster empathy and understanding within your team.

4. Practice mindfulness: Mindfulness helps increase emotional intelligence by promoting self-awareness and helping people manage their emotions.

Entrepreneurship is inherently filled with ups and downs. By developing emotional intelligence, you can navigate business challenges with resilience, build meaningful relationships with team members and customers, and lead your business towards success. Your emotional intelligence is a fundamental entrepreneurial tool, so start honing it today.

Chapter 7. Resilience and Recovery: Lessons from Successful Entrepreneurs

In the world of entrepreneurship, both resilience and recovery are essential. These twin aspects form the foundation on which successful entrepreneurs build their empires. Encountering failures, facing adversity, and experiencing business upheavals, they embark on the path to success – a path paved with resilience and an unwavering will to recover.

7.1. The Power of Resilience

Resilience is a term that has its roots in the Latin word "resilire," which means "to leap back." In the context of entrepreneurship, resilience refers to the entrepreneurs' ability to withstand the unpredicted storms of the business terrain and bounce back.

Every entrepreneurial journey is unique, yet all are strewn with similar challenges – uncertainty, risk, failure. The success of a venture depends significantly on how entrepreneurs navigate through these adversities.

Successful entrepreneurs such as Bill Gates, Steve Jobs, and Elon Musk have demonstrated resilience in their entrepreneurial journeys. For instance, before co-founding Apple, Steve Jobs was devastated when he was removed from his own company. Yet, he leveraged his resilience, founded NeXT, and eventually returned to Apple as its CEO, leading to its restoration as a profitable enterprise.

There are several factors that contribute to cultivating resilience among entrepreneurs. These might include a positive outlook, a flexible attitude, the ability to manage stress, a strong support network, and possessing a high level of self-esteem. Training and developing these key characteristics can significantly amplify an individual's resilience.

7.2. Recovery and its Significance

Recovery is intrinsically linked with resilience but is a distinct concept. If resilience is about withstanding pressure, recovery is about bouncing back post damage or disturbance.

Failure in entrepreneurship is inevitable; even the most notable entrepreneurial figures have met with failure at some point. For instance, before his success with SpaceX and Tesla, Elon Musk's first web software company, Zip2, was initially a difficult sell.

How entrepreneurs perceive, handle, and learn from failures paves their path towards recovery and ultimately, success. Adopting a growth mindset, seeing failure as a learning tool, and maintaining perseverance in the face of setbacks are crucial for a strong recovery approach.

7.3. Resilience and Recovery: A Synergistic Relationship

While resilience and recovery are distinct facets, their intertwined existence fosters entrepreneurial tenacity. It's similar to a muscle that strengthens with consistent exercise. The more you practice resilience and recovery, the stronger you become in handling the ebbs and flows of entrepreneurship.

For instance, Colonel Sanders, the founder of KFC, faced countless rejections for his fried chicken recipe before it finally caught on. Had he not demonstrated resilience and recovery, KFC would not have become the global brand it is today.

Resilience lets entrepreneurs endure challenges and maintain stability despite setbacks. Meanwhile, recovery aids in getting back on track post disturbance, enabling entrepreneurs to learn from their missteps and utilize setbacks as stepping stones towards success.

7.4. Building Resilience: Strategies and Techniques

Building resilience is a journey rather than a destination. Here are few methodologies to help foster resilience:

1. Foster a positive attitude: Encourage optimism and block out the negative noise. Turning challenges into opportunities can significantly fuel resilience.

2. Build a strong support network: Relationships play a crucial role in enhancing resilience. Engage with mentors, peers, or supportive friends who can guide you.

3. Prioritize Self-Care: Managing physical health and mental wellbeing is crucial. Regular exercise, balanced diet, and ample sleep can boost resilience.

4. Embrace change: Flexibility is a key attribute of resilience. With an ever-changing business landscape, readiness to adapt ensures survival and growth.

7.5. Embracing Recovery: Tools and Tactics

Recovery also requires a specific set of strategies:

1. Adopt a growth mindset: See failures as opportunities for learning and growth. Encourage experimentation and innovation, nurturing an environment where failures are

stepping stones.

2. Leverage reflection: Post failure, it's crucial to reflect on what went wrong and why. Unpack your experiences, learn from them and adapt your actions accordingly.

3. Seek Feedback: Convert criticism into constructive feedback for improvement. The right feedback can give valuable insights for necessary changes.

4. Implement Rehabilitation: Put in place recovery methods to ensure you bounce back stronger.

In conclusion, resilience and recovery together act as pillars to entrepreneurial success. Building and maintaining these attributes foster a robust entrepreneurial mindset, contributing significantly to long-term business success. These are not innate characters but skills that need honing over time. So, get started on your journey to resilience and recovery now, and step closer to your entrepreneurial dream!

Chapter 8. Creative Problem-Solving in Entrepreneurship

Entrepreneurship is a journey filled with challenges and obstacles. But take heart! Within those challenges lie opportunities for growth and innovation. The art of creative problem-solving is a fundamental skill that can transform these hurdles into stepping stones to success. This process involves identifying, analyzing, exploring, and ultimately, making effective decisions that will shape the trajectory of your venture.

8.1. The Importance of Creative Problem-Solving

The world of entrepreneurship is a dynamic one that is always in flux. Changes in market trends, customer preferences, technology, and industry innovation can bring about complex issues that require much more than routine solutions.

Being equipped with creative problem-solving skills allows you to think outside the box and come up with unique, innovative solutions. Furthermore, this skill primes you to see the silver lining behind every problem, viewing them as opportunities to improve and innovate.

Stimulating creativity promotes cognitive flexibility, making you adaptable in an ever-changing entrepreneurial landscape.

8.2. Walking Through the Creative Problem-Solving Process

Creative problem-solving isn't just stumbled upon; it is crafted. It's a structured process that, when understood and leveraged, can bring forth surprising solutions.

1. **Identification:** Begin by recognizing that a problem exists. Don't shy away from challenges. Instead, take a step back, understand the intricacy of the issue, and frame it in a way that it presents itself as an opportunity instead of a roadblock.

2. **Information Gathering:** Comprehensive research is the key. Delve into the details of the problem while scanning your surroundings for similar issues and their solutions. Learn from past experiences, industry case studies and market trends.

3. **Idea Generation:** Allow your creative juices to flow. Traditional brainstorming, lateral thinking, and other creativity-enhancing techniques can help you generate a plethora of solutions.

4. **Experimentation:** After selecting a few promising ideas, test their feasibility. Simulate real-world conditions to evaluate the effectiveness of each solution.

5. **Implementation:** Put your chosen solution to work and monitor its performance. Be prepared to refine your solution based on the feedback and results it generates.

8.3. Techniques for Enhancing Creative Problem-Solving

Here are some effective tools for enhancing your creative problem-solving skills.

1. **Mind Mapping:** This technique helps visually organize information, allowing for the free-flow of ideas and fostering understanding of complex issues.

2. **Brainstorming:** An old but gold method for idea generation. It requires an open, non-judgmental environment where any and every idea is welcome.

3. **SWOT Analysis:** Identifying an issue's Strengths, Weaknesses, Opportunities, and Threats can throw light on potential solutions.

4. **Six Thinking Hats:** This is a time-tested technique where different perspectives (represented by six different color hats) are taken to evaluate a problem and its potential solutions.

8.4. Real-Life Examples of Creative Problem-Solving in Entrepreneurship

Nothing validates theory more than real-life applications. Let us now delve into some inspiring examples of how entrepreneurs used creative problem-solving to leapfrog challenges.

1. Netflix: Its subscription-based model disrupted the traditional rental business. With a creative problem-solving approach, they redefined their industry, evolving from DVD rentals to a streaming behemoth.

2. Airbnb: At a time when the team was struggling with finances, they creatively solved their problem by selling custom-designed cereal boxes during the 2008 U.S. presidential election. This not only raised enough capital but also attracted investor attention, turning their fortunes around.

By mastering creative problem-solving, you can carve innovative paths through challenges and steer your venture into unchartered territories of success and growth. Entrepreneurs need to foster a culture where every problem is seen as a creator of opportunities and every solution a step towards innovation. Reignite your entrepreneurial journey with the power-packed combination of creativity and problem-solving.

Chapter 9. Fostering Leadership and Teamwork for Business Success

When a novice athlete enrolls into a professional sports training academy, they don't commence a game the very next day; instead, they invest significant time in mastering basic skills before they progress to more complicated maneuvers. This principle is equally applicable in the sphere of business leadership and teamwork. Effective leadership is a skill that can be honed, and is a fundamental element that goes hand in hand with assembling and managing a high-performing team successfully.

9.1. The Crux of Leadership in Entrepreneurship

Leadership in entrepreneurship is not simply about holding a position or having people work under your supervision. It's about inspiring others to believe in your vision, and working together towards a common aim. The most successful entrepreneurs possess an innate ability to influence their subordinates in a way that propels the entire team forward. Through their words, behaviors, and actions, leaders can make a meaningful difference in the daily lives of their teams and the growth trajectory of the organization.

First and foremost, leaders should present a clear vision. A leader provides guidance, setting both short-term and long-term goals for the team. These goals serve as the building blocks towards the ultimate vision of success. By clearly articulating and communicating these goals, leaders stringently align their teams with the organization's mission and pathway to success.

9.2. Building a High-performance Team

The saying "two heads are better than one" holds much wisdom in the business domain. The process of building a high-performing team begins with hiring the right people. Always remember that skills can be taught but attitude cannot. Hire for attitude, and train for skill.

Once the right team is hired, invest time in creating a positive environment conducive to open communication, creativity, and collaboration. Fostering an atmosphere that spurs innovation can be your competitive edge in the ever-dynamic business landscape.

9.3. Building Trust: The Foundation of Effective Leadership and Teamwork

Trust, though a simple five-lettered word, holds colossal importance in the realms of leadership and teamwork. A high trust environment steers clear of hidden agendas, fosters open dialogue, encourages collaboration, and minimizes uncertainty. Leaders should take the responsibility to cultivate trust by being open, honest, consistent, and reliable.

9.4. The Power of Inclusion

The power of inclusion cannot be overstated. When everyone on the team feels valued, there's a significant jump in productivity levels, job satisfaction, and commitment to the organization. Leaders need to demonstrate respect for diverse viewpoints, recognize individual achievements, and encourage participation in decision making.

9.5. The Role of Empathy in Leadership

Empathy enables a leader to genuinely understand the conflicts and motivations of their team on a deeper, more intuitive level. This understanding fosters stronger connections, which can directly enhance the team's productivity and morale. By being empathetic, leaders can model a culture that promotes mental well-being and open communication, propelling the team towards success.

9.6. Encouraging Risk-Taking

Entrepreneurial leaders keen on pushing the envelope should foster a culture of risk-taking. By nurturing this culture, leaders encourage their teams to step outside their comfort zones, innovate, and come up with out-of-the-box solutions.

While risks come with the territory of potential failure, they also open doors for substantial growth. Leaders must ensure that failure isn't demonized in the organization, instead it should be seen as a stepping stone to success, an opportunity for learning and improvement.

9.7. Promoting Continuous Learning and Development

The growth of an organization is directly proportional to the growth of its people. As such, organizations must cultivate a culture of continuous learning and development. Leaders can encourage their team to acquire new skills, keeping them abreast of industry trends, ultimately making the organization adaptable and future-proof.

Leadership and teamwork are inseparable aspects of organizational success. Whether you are starting a new venture or trying to scale an existing business, fostering leadership and teamwork will underpin a solid foundation for your long-term success. Your ability to inspire and work cooperatively with your team holds the key to unlock unlimited entrepreneurial success. Steer your venture in the right direction by investing in leadership and teamwork. Today is the perfect day to take that first step towards transforming your vision into reality.

Chapter 10. Entrepreneurial Ethics and Integrity

In the world of entrepreneurship, ethics and integrity are more than just desirable traits – they are fundamental prerequisites for sustainable success. A business driven by ethical considerations transcends beyond just profits, focusing on creating value that benefits all. Coupled with integrity, ethics breed trust – the key to long-term significance and impact in any industry.

10.1. The Importance of Ethics and Integrity

Ethics, in essence, are moral principles that guide individuals' behavior or conduct. Entrepreneurial ethics, therefore, is the value system specially designed for entrepreneurs that aids them in making choices that are morally correct or acceptable. Having a solid ethical foundation in entrepreneurship ensures that you conduct your business with honesty and respect for stakeholders, thus fostering trust and establishing a positive reputation.

Conversely, integrity is the quality of being honest and demonstrating unwavering moral principles. For entrepreneurs, integrity is reflected in honoring commitments, doing the right thing even when no one is watching, and standing by their word even in challenging circumstances. It is one of the most important attributes an entrepreneur can have, as it attracts loyal customers and passionate employees.

Entrepreneurs with both ethics and integrity are adept at navigating their ventures through ethical dilemmas, and in the process, they create businesses that stand the test of time. When these entrepreneurs face situations that challenge their moral fabric, they prioritize what is right over what is easy or profitable.

10.2. Developing Ethical Mindset

To incorporate ethics and integrity into your entrepreneurial journey, it's essential to develop an ethical mindset. This mindset involves being willing and able to reflect on the implications of your actions and decisions, then committing to choose the most ethical path – even when it's not the most convenient or profitable.

Ethical entrepreneurs practice reflection regularly, continually assessing their decisions and actions for alignment with their ethical values. Reflection is a powerful tool for personal growth, and it allows entrepreneurs to identify opportunities for ethical improvements in their businesses. The power of reflection also enables entrepreneurs to recognize when they've erred and to learn from their mistakes so these are not repeated.

Developing an ethical mindset also requires courage. As an entrepreneur, it takes bravery to face ethical dilemmas head-on and choose the ethical path, even when it may lead to temporary losses or setbacks. However, making these courageous, ethical choices will benefit your venture in the long run by establishing your reputation as a trustworthy and principled business.

10.3. Integrity as a Business Advantage

While integrity is a central part of personal character, it also serves as a competitive advantage for businesses. Companies founded on integrity operate with transparency, honesty, empathy, and accountability, both internally and externally.

Businesses with genuine integrity make influential industry leaders as they inspire trust. A company viewed as trustworthy will have an easier time attracting and retaining customers, clients, and talented staff.

Integrity also helps promote responsible decision-making. When business leaders model integrity, they motivate their team to adhere to the same high standards. This culture of integrity can result in better decisions, as employees factor ethics into their decision-making process.

10.4. Ethical Leadership

In the entrepreneurial context, leadership is more than running a business – it's about inspiring people to believe in your vision and guiding them toward achieving shared goals. Such leadership becomes extraordinarily influential when it is steeped in ethics and integrity.

Ethical leadership means leading by example and demonstrating ethical behavior in all activities, decisions, and interactions. It's about holding yourself accountable and owning up to mistakes, as well as adhering to a consistent set of moral principles and values.

Ethical leaders inspire trust, motivate individuals to excel, and build a workplace culture that upholds ethical behavior as a standard. Employees who witness ethical leadership are more likely to emulate it, thereby creating a ripple-effect that reinforces and spreads ethical practices throughout the organization.

10.5. Conclusion

Strong ethics and integrity are the pillars upon which successful businesses are built. By integrating these values into your day-to-day operations, you foster trust and respect among your stakeholders, reinforce a positive brand image, and set your venture on a path towards sustainable success. The journey to entrepreneurship is filled with complexities, but with an ethical mindset and unwavering integrity, entrepreneurs can separate themselves from the competition and build businesses that are truly impactful and enduring.

Chapter 11. Cultivating a Growth Mindset for Sustainable Success

The inherent complexity of entrepreneurship demands more than just technical skills and business acumen. Central to this is your mindset which dramatically impacts the course and outcome of all your endeavors. Hence, cultivating a growth mindset is one of the fundamental steps you should embark upon on your entrepreneurial journey

11.1. The Definition and Importance of a Growth Mindset

As proposed by Stanford psychologist Carol Dweck, one's mindset can be sorted into two categories: fixed and growth. Persons with a fixed mindset perceive their abilities as static, immutable aspects of themselves, stifling growth and improvement. On the other hand, adopting a growth mindset involves an acknowledgement that abilities and intelligence can be developed, thereby paving the way for constant learning, challenges, and ultimately, personal and professional advancement.

In the context of entrepreneurship, a growth mindset is equally, if not more, crucial. To weather the storm of uncertainties and challenges that start-ups often encounter, a growth mindset helps you embrace failures, learn from mistakes, and continuously evolve in sync with changing market dynamics.

11.2. Cultivating a Growth Mindset: Where to Begin?

Understanding the importance of a growth mindset is the first step. What follows is the gradual and consistent cultivation of the same. Here's how to get started:

1. Embrace Challenges: It's only natural for you to encounter challenges in your entrepreneurial journey. Instead of feeling overwhelmed or deterred, it's important to shift your perspective and consider these as opportunities for learning and testing your resilience.

2. Learn from Criticism: Feedback, particularly negative, can be hard to swallow. But a key aspect of a growth mindset involves leveraging criticism as a source of insights for improvement.

3. Be Inspired by Others' Success: Some may view peers' success as a threat, but a growth mindset prompts you to be inspired and learn from their journeys.

4. Patience and Persistence: Shifting the mindset isn't an overnight affair. It requires constant effort and the will to persist. Remember, the core of a growth mindset lies in the belief that long term development is possible and worth the effort.

11.3. Embracing Failures, Learning from Mistakes

Mistakes and failures can weigh heavy on anyone, especially entrepreneurs who are closely tied to their ventures. However, with a growth mindset, these apparent setbacks are reframed as valuable learning opportunities. By assessing what went wrong, why it happened, and how it could be prevented, you empower yourself to evolve and improve. Each failure is transformed into a stepping-stone, guiding you towards better decision-making and strategies in the future.

11.4. Emphasizing Continuous Learning and Skill Development

A growth mindset places a premium on continuous learning, which is vital in the fast-paced entrepreneurial world. Make it a point to update your knowledge constantly, learn new skills, attend workshops, seminars, and engage in peer learning. Learning is a lifelong process, and a growth mindset ensures you make the most of every opportunity to gain and apply the knowledge.

11.5. Growth Mindset and Resilience: The Perfect Pair

The trajectory of an entrepreneur's journey is filled with ups and downs, hence resilience is paramount. The cultivation of a growth mindset goes hand-in-hand with fostering resilience. By viewing challenges as opportunities and failures as learning experiences, the harsh bumps of the entrepreneurial path are softened, and your resilience is strengthened.

11.6. Manifesting a Growth Mindset in Business Practices

A growth mindset isn't limited to overcoming personal challenges but also extends to how you manage and run your venture. With this mindset, you can foster a culture of innovation, encourage feedback, adapt quickly to change, and be more experimental with your strategies. Your team feeds off your energy. Showing them the benefits of a growth mindset will pay dividends in productivity and morale.

11.7. Summary: The Growth Mindset, Entrepreneurship's Secret Ingredient

In sum, cultivating a growth mindset can significantly enhance your entrepreneurial capacities. By viewing abilities as developable, embracing failures as lessons, and perpetually seeking opportunities for learning, your footing on the entrepreneurship ladder is more than solidified. It's the secret ingredient that adds a resilient backbone to your business, guiding you through thick and thin towards sustainable entrepreneurial success.

Remember, the journey towards cultivating a growth mindset is slow and gradual, often just as much as the entrepreneurial journey itself. But equipped with resilience and fortified by a belief in learnability, the road less traveled will certainly make all the difference. Celebrate every step forward, every lesson learned, and every challenge surmounted. After all, entrepreneurship isn't just about the destination – it's about the journey.

www.ingramcontent.com/pod-product-compliance
Lightning Source LLC
Chambersburg PA
CBHW062310290526
45794CB00006B/2744